Chief No Feathers Presents:

Another Day on the Yukon

By LMB Wordsmith
(Chief No Feathers)

Chief No Feathers Presents:

Another Day on the Yukon

Table of Contents

~ 4 ~

Another Day On The Yukon

America has always been a land of immigrants.

It's just that some immigrants have been here longer than others.   And on that basis, claim some supremacy over subsequent arrivals.

But we all originated from the same place – somewhere else.

*****

But the question remains: So why did Asians reach the Americas before the Europeans?   Well, simply, because they walked here.

Just because 12,000 years later Europeans came from another direction and called these Asians "Indians" doesn't change the facts regarding where they came from, or when, or how.

*****

The Klondike runs north into the Yukon River in Canada, and then the Yukon River heads northwest into Alaska up to Fort Yukon, where it turns southwest and heads out to the Pacific about a thousand miles later.

The Porcupine River also heads west out of Canada, before turning south where it joins the Yukon at the Fort – which is why the Russians, the English, and the Hudson Bay Trading Company set up a trading post there.

*****

Indian Reservation Roads (IRR) helps tribes with roads – getting the funding for the roads as well as providing engineering assistance. Tribes get money from IRR based on the number of miles of road they have in their inventory. The definition of "road" is quite loose. It has to be when you are talking about Alaska. (Also see "Navigable Waters", a legal term, but, again, different when it comes to Alaska.)

So "road" can mean water [in its liquid form], as it is in Southeast Alaska, and parts of the Alaska Marine Highway. It could mean a boardwalk, which is all one village had (as in Pelican).   Or it could be an "ice road" [water in its solid form], which is what we were trying to do up at the Fort on the Yukon one winter.

The Alaska Marine Highway pulling into a Native Village

Main Street (in Pelican, Alaska)

High Noon on the Yukon (December above the Arctic Circle)

*****

There were trees downriver that could be harvested for fuel to keep tribal members' homes heated during the winter [N: It didn't get warmer than -40 degrees Fahrenheit for months during the winter (it was actually colder, but my thermometer only went down to -40)].

For what happens when it gets even colder, see "When It Goes Below -65 Degrees".

So to drive a CAT (a Caterpillar tractor) on ice, IRR said the ice had to be at least 10" thick. I had my roads guy go out on the Yukon to take borings to measure the thickness, and then to place flags out there so people knew where it is safe to drive [likewise, in Fairbanks by the Lodge that is the northern Starting Line for the Iditarod ["The Last Great Race on Earth"] when there is not enough snow in Anchorage [what?! – no snow in Anchorage? – say it ain't so Joe!]], people cross the river there in Fairbanks during the winter. But I don't know if anyone takes ice borings at that crossing.   Locals tell me there are several cars and a bunch of trucks though at the bottom of the river just outside the Lodge].

Jack had come into my office to say he wanted to drive a CAT down the Yukon to get some logs.

~ Fine, I said – but we [the Tribe] don't have a CAT.

~ I know, he said, but the Native Corporation does. [Most Natives in Alaska are members of a Tribe and of a Native Corporation (actually, two Native Corporations – one for their village and one for their region [see, in part, "Henry (Brains, Guts & Charm)" as well as "His Name Was 'Cowboy' " and "Eating Between Two Sharks"]).]

~ Borrow it, he says, from the Native Corporation[1].

~ If I do, Jack, I want you to promise me you will have someone walking behind you with a radio or cell phone [which actually work sporadically up there – better than, say, out beyond Possum Trot in the Ozarks].

~ Of course, he says, and leaves.

Well, I used to run a Native Corporation, and know the lady in charge of this one. So I call her up, and arrange to rent the CAT from them.

✱✱✱✱✱

A couple of days later Jack returns. The Native Corporation has delivered the key to their CAT to me. As I hand the key to Jack, I again ask if he has someone with a radio or cell phone to walk behind him?

~ Of course, he says.

✱✱✱✱✱

---

[1] Here is where the complexity of humans and their governments and their corporations come in [I didn't learn this till later] but Jack and the Native Corporation [of which he was a Native shareholder] did not, let's say, get along [it's more serious, but doesn't matter here].

The location is now known as "Jack's Point".

Jack's CAT in the Yukon.

It took several other CAT's and a number of attempts, with nearly all the men in the village present, before Jack's CAT got first onto dry ice and then onto dry land.

He still had a sense of humor as of last night. We were standing together when they finally got the CAT out of the river and onto dry ice. He said he was ready to try this again tomorrow . . . if anyone else would lend him another CAT (!)

The mechanics dragged this CAT back through town, and pushed it into a warm garage. The news keeps getting better. Yesterday, I thought the town had just been hit with a $50,000 loss, and who would bear it?: The Tribe? Jack? The Native Corporation which lent us its CAT?

Today, the mechanics are draining out the fluids. The engine may be fine (!) They want to replace the electrical gear (e.g., the alternator) because it was under water.

And no one is blaming anyone (at least not yet); they all seem to be taking this in stride – just another day on the Yukon.

*****

Our transportation guy had done ice borings on the Yukon. The scientists/road engineers at IRR had said the ice should be at least 10" thick. The ice borings revealed it was about 24" thick, so we had a safety margin of at least 2 times the minimum. Jack had driven heavy equipment successfully in this area for the last 4 years. He said he knew how to "read the ice".

I had just spoken to Jack less than an hour before I got the news of the sinking of the CAT. I had specifically asked if he would have someone watching/trailing him, and he assured me he would. [He didn't.]

Jack was fortunately not wearing a seat belt when the accident occurred. Otherwise, he may not have been able to get out in time in the freezing, rushing waters of the Yukon. As it was, he didn't even have time to turn off the engine.

He was however able to escape and scramble out of the water in time.

He couldn't turn off the engine in the rush of the sinking, so the battery glow light was sending out a reddish pink glow from under the water.

Alaska Native Health is dragging the CAT back through the town to a shop so the water doesn't freeze in the engine and cause even more problems.

The mechanics in town will work on the CAT in the morning.

Tomorrow at noon we have a telephonic conference with the Feds about our transportation projects - including the ice road - which is what Jack was running on when he crashed through the ice.

It is interesting to see how the town responded. We'll be hosting a lunch for the men, as most were out there just to help.

*****

Horace Greeley, the editor of the New York Tribune, liked to say: "Go West, young man, and grow up with the country."

Jack's father, a former First Chief, likes to take credit (on behalf of all Gwich'in) for populating all of North America south of the Yukon [as well as all of South America]. As succeeding bands of "Indians" (all pioneering Asians themselves) crossed the Bering Land Bridge [when the sea levels were lower (because the receding ice sheets had not yet melted enough to fill the area between Siberia and Alaska with [liquid] water)], the Gwich'in told these later arrivals over The Bridge to "keep moving!"

So all the new immigrants to North America, presaging Horace Greeley's famous dicta by millennia, were urged to:

~ Go South, you brave people – __keep moving!__

[This is part of the "Cowboy Trilogy"; the other parts are "Cowboy's Niece" and "Eating Between Two Sharks".]

His Name Was "Cowboy"

For perspective: sometime before I became General Manager of a Native corporation in Southeast Alaska, I heard of another Native corporation which had had a white manager which had just encountered a business fiasco. As he started the meeting, he apparently said: "It's time to circle the wagons" [a good defensive move, but apparently this phrase sent the Natives into a tizzy].

With this as prologue, I was quite surprised when I saw and heard the following—

His name was "Cowboy".

He was a Gwich'in who was killed on the North Slope while working as a roustabout on an oil well for a nearby Native corporation, when a heavy steel pipe swung around and smashed his skull.

After being flown to Anchorage for an autopsy, they flew him in a casket back to the Fort. I let them use one of the tribe's trucks with the thought they would move the casket from the plane to the truck, and then drive over to the church. Instead, with a beautiful, hand carved, 12' cross leading the way (see above photograph), the men (his friends and family) carried the Gwich'in Indian themselves from the plane, past the tribal truck, and through town to the church, where they went in and placed him with reverence and respect up by the altar.

The next day, the funeral service was held at the high school gym (as with most Alaska villages, the largest room in town). The preacher lady was a Gwich'in from Old Crow _[in the Yukon in Canada; we were on the Yukon in Alaska]_.

Near the end, the preacher lady came down from the lectern, looked under the drape over the coffin, and read the carving on the coffin: "Cowboy". She said Davey always liked to be a cowboy – because cowboys were always on the winning side.

    ~ _But you know, she said, they always [as she smacked her chest] shot us Indians._

~ So go out there and be cowboys, be on the winning side, but don't forget where you came from, and don't forget your Indian roots!

    – God Bless!

<u>Cowboy's Niece</u>

At one point during the funeral for Cowboy, time was set aside for one of his nieces (perhaps in her 20's) to read a poem she had written about her uncle. It was clear, at least to me, from the precision of her words, the pictures, the atmosphere, the emotions generated, that she was a poet.

*****

A couple of hours after the funeral was held at the school gym, we had a potlatch at the Tribal Hall.

Before the food was ready, there was a mingling of people, guests, family and tribal members. I saw the niece, and went over to her. I thanked her for her beautiful ode to Cowboy, to her uncle.

I suspected she wasn't a neophyte at writing, so asked her how long she had been writing poetry.

She said: ~ Oh, about 10 or 15 years.

[I had thought so.]

— How long did it take to write that poem, I asked.

~ About 10 minutes, she replied.

[I had thought 15 minutes.]

But that is how the Muses work: a lifetime of knowledge, of thought, comes out in a creative burst. At that point, we are merely conduits. We merely hold the pen.

[Of course, you need the 10-15 years (or half a century) first before you become a "mere conduit".]

Eating Between Two Sharks

The CEO of Cowboy's employer, the Regional Native Corporation, came to town for his (Cowboy's) funeral.

How many CEO's attend the funeral of employees who are killed while working for their company?

The CEO came in his best buckskin.

He came alone.

He sat alone.

*****

I actually thought it took a significant amount of personal bravery for the CEO even to come to our town [he wouldn't, for example, come – even though invited – when our U.S. Senator was making a special trip to the Fort].

The Natives in this town, while they were among the shareholders of the regional corporation he represented and was responsible for, were well known for actively opposing both him and the corporation on some of the most important development projects the corporation was undertaking.

It is a tension that **may never** get resolved.

It is a tension that perhaps **should never** get resolved.

It is the tension of developing resources, of exploring (in this case) for and, if found, producing oil and/or gas [to bring in money to advance the economic well-being of its Native shareholders and employees] **VERSUS** the subsistence rights and mores of the those same Natives who actually live and survive on the fruit, the meat, the birds, the berries and the fish that walk, fly over, or swim on that land. It is what has kept them alive for over 10,000 years ever since their ancestors first walked across The Bridge[2] – the Bering Land Bridge that once connected Asia to the Americas.

> [Remember too – Cowboy was killed in the quest for oil on an oil derrick on the North Slope less than a week earlier.]

This CEO was the person I had proposed meeting when I was taking my first trip to Fairbanks on behalf of the Tribe [faster than one can say "Hell no!", I learned about the tension and animosity between these two Native organizations, the Indian Tribe and this Native Corporation].

---

[2] Also see "Another Day On The Yukon" [for the succeeding bands of Asians to "keep moving!"] — so all the new immigrants to North America (presaging Horace Greeley's famous dicta by millennia) were urged to: ~ Go South, you brave people – keep moving!

✳✳✳✳✳

After the Cowboy's funeral service at the school gym, we hosted a potlatch for his family and the community at the Tribal Hall.

Family and friends arrived by plane, unless they came by boat on the Yukon [there are no roads to the Fort].

I was sitting and talking with a council member of the civil government at the Fort [I was in charge of the tribal government[3]]. At some point, he went up to get on the long line that led to the tables and tables of food.

After awhile, I got up to get to the end of that very long line. I got a plate of caribou, a tidbit of moose, a breast of wild duck, and a couple of Yukon Gold potatoes.

When I returned to our table, the CEO, who already had a plate of food, was sitting on the bench across the table from the council member.

The council member knew I was an attorney; he apparently knew the CEO's professional credentials too.

In introducing me to the CEO, he said – *with a glint in his eyes*: "I always wondered what it would be like to eat between two sharks."

---

[3] For more on Tribal Government, see "The Pentagon Wants Its Bombs Back" as well as "The New & Improved Poisoned Blanket Policy".

When It Goes Below -65 Degrees

I thought I knew the cold. After all, I had already spent two winters in Barrow at the northern tip of Alaska [see "& The Answer Is ___________" and "A Rough Way To Teach A Kid"] years earlier.

But at The Fort, for every 20 degrees it got colder, the worse it got.

At -20 degrees, it was simply cold, very cold.

At -40 degrees, it just plain hurt.

But at -60 degrees, the moisture in my throat froze – so that my throat felt dry, which thus caused my body to go into coughing fits in a futile attempt to bring mucous or moisture up into it. Failing that, my asthma kicked in seriously. [Asthma inhibits one's ability to breathe by closing up the bronchial tubes which carry air into one's lungs. If one can't breathe – one dies. It is really quite simple.[4]   (Thousands do it [die] each year.)]

On a Saturday morning, when the temperature was someplace south of -65 degrees (and so much like the sun which was south of the horizon), I decided to go down to the Tribal Hall to check, and to help as needed, to see if it had heat. [For elsewhere in Alaska at the same time, see "Eat or Heat?" in "The Crab Pot Theory Of Tlingit Society".]

And there was also the question of Tribal Members, but they were already being helped or assisted by my staff.

Tribal Members heat their homes using wood with wood stoves and/or with oil using oil heaters. If they use oil, they usually have a 50 gallon oil drum perched on some kind of support just outside of their house. The oil drum is usually a couple of inches higher than the level of the oil heater inside the house – so the oil can get to it by gravity feed. The oil drum and the oil heater are generally connected by a piece of ¼ inch copper tubing.

Generally, it works fine.

But at -65 degrees, the oil in the copper tubing congeals (one state short of freezing, but it has the same effect: the oil doesn't move or flow).

Without oil flowing to the oil heater, the heater is useless; it doesn't work; and the Indians inside get very cold [but they are survivors (they've been that way for millennia – since long before their ancestors crossed the Bering Land Bridge), so they will work things out].

*****

Though my Tribal Truck had been plugged in all night [by an electric cord to an engine block heater], I was still (at someplace below -65 degrees below zero) having trouble getting it to turn over and start.

---

[4] See "A Sickly Lad"   [Theodore Roosevelt].

The Tribal Truck and my cabin with its Arctic Entry Way entrance at The Fort

I looked over to one of my neighbors, a Half Breed, who was having more luck than me with his truck. I went over to him. He needed to get into town to the shop he worked at for something he was responsible for, and he agreed to bring me into town to check the Tribal Hall   [as a half breed, while looked down upon by the FBI [Full Blooded Indian][5], he was still a Tribal Member].

His shop was fine [its heating system was still working], and we then went over to the Tribal Hall. One of my employees had already come in, had un-froze the oil in the copper tubing, and had restored heating to the Tribal Hall.

Other employees had come in on this weekend to work, and so the various Tribal Members who were having problems with heat were being taken care of.

My neighbor decided to then take me out to "White Alice".

"White Alice" is the successor to our "DEW" line – The Distant Early Warning system that was originally set up to detect Russian nuclear bombers coming in over the Arctic Ocean to

---

[5] See "FBI In The Neighborhood".

attack North America.   "White Alice" is used to detect Russian ballistic nuclear weapons traversing roughly the same course to attack North America.[6]

And in conjunction with King George and his Good Friend Dick's program to divert federal (public) money to their private friends and campaign contributors [see "Patriot or Terrorist?"], "White Alice" national defense is now run, operated and manned by private defense contractors – Oh What?!!!

On the way back to town, my neighbor points out the various animal tracks that cross or parallel the road, and tells me which animal made which track.

Back in town we go to the gas station: it is closed.

> At -65 degrees, the gasoline pumps at the village's sole gas station froze, so no one could get gas, and were stuck with whatever gas they still had in their tank from the night before. [*Of course, having gas in the tank only mattered if one could actually start the engine to one's vehicle.*]

But Life continues at The Fort.

It has for millennia, millennia before Europe ever dreamed of (much less "found") North America.   With luck[7], fortitude and the perseverance that has kept them alive for over 10,000 years, it will continue.

---

[6] See "**& THAT**, My Friends, Is Tactical Surprise!" for perspective.

[7] See "Us Gray Hairs" on "luck".

Food Stamps

They don't issue food stamps in this remote area of Alaska.

They would be fairly worthless, like Confederate money: food available in the one store the village may have is prohibitively expensive, so the food stamps wouldn't go far.

And because of the distance [which then translates into time] the food has to travel, it's not fresh.

Unless one works for the government, there are very few jobs for which one can earn cash.

So if you qualify for food stamps, what they hand you instead are rifle cartridges or shotgun shells, and it's up to you to bring home the food for your family.

It's Called Ruby Tuesday Because It's Bloody Tuesday

Made it to Fairbanks.

*****

I've heard of people who wouldn't take "No" for an answer, but I never met one (till now) who wouldn't take "Yes" or "Yes, Ma'am, It's Done!" for an answer.

*****

Tribal Council meetings were normally held in the evening, but we had a special one before the upcoming Tanana Chiefs Conference in Fairbanks during the day on Tuesday.

After the Tribal Council meeting, the 1st Chief came in to my office.

She ripped into me to get [something] done!

I knew **the proper answer** is: ~ Yes, ma'am, I will.

But instead I told her **the truthful answer**: ~ Yes, ma'am, I have.

And I pointed to the folder I had given her, wherein I had advised her and the whole Tribal Council last weekend that I had already done [that] last week.

She didn't want to hear it!

~ Do it!

– But I have.

~ Do it!

– But I have. If you read the first sentence of my letter to you, you'll see that I've already done it.

~ Do it! she yelled again. Some people won't take "No" for an answer. The 1st Chief just wasn't going to take "Yes, ma'am, but I've done it!" for an answer.

She wouldn't hear any more. She stormed out my door, shouting.

*****

My "Acting Executive Director" when I'm out of town, who knew parts of what had happened this afternoon (probably from the 1st Chief's shouting in the hallway), also knew I had to drop the tribal truck off to get it fixed.

So in late afternoon, I met her at the truck shop with the Tribal Operations lady – I said bring me to the airport.

They did, but they were both aghast that I had decided to say "Hell with it!", and leave The Fort tonight.

*****

I told them no, not yet, but that I had to meet the Alaska Energy Authority tomorrow in Fairbanks, and I'd be back. We were to fly out to several villages which had renewable energy projects that were actually operating and viable.

Alaska – at an altitude most "Outsiders" never get to fly.

Most Native villages, including The Fort, are still on diesel, which is costly, problematic, and hazardous (considering how and when it is transported).[8]

The Tribal Ops lady said I needed a "sho____", but I didn't catch the word. I thought she said "shock", as in I needed "electric shock treatment" to my brain.

She repeated: "shot", as she threw her head back with her hand to her mouth – "You need a shot [of whiskey]!"

[Also see, when you have the heart, "Crossing Swords".]

____

[8] See "Eat or Heat" in "The Crab Pot Theory Of Tlingit Society".

Crossing Swords

Preface: Different cultures look at and do things differently. See, e.g., "Dulles International Airport" [Japanese] or "Brown Paper Bag" [Black Americans]. Here's how another culture does things.

The First Chief had asked me to contact a group that could assist the Tribe in certain planning the Tribe wished to do.

I did.

I spoke with this group and arranged for their telephonic appearance before the Tribal Council, to be followed up with a trip to The Fort to see the village and to meet the Tribal Council in person.

I set this all out, as events and news developed, in memos and emails to the First Chief and the rest of the Tribal Council to keep them apprised of what I was doing.

The first telephonic conference didn't occur because the phone company's operators couldn't get the phone call in to us at The Fort.

The second telephonic conference didn't occur because, while I had put it on the agenda, the First Chief canceled the appearance and deleted the item from the agenda.

The Tribe always had a table of food, whether snacks, potlatch, or dishes tribal members had made to share at these meetings.

At one point in the meeting, the First Chief started talking, got up and went over to the table for a bite of something. As she was returning to her seat, she told everyone at this public meeting (tribal members as well as the Tribal Council) that she had told me to contact this group – and that I hadn't (!)

Well, if this had been a closed meeting of just the Tribal Council (rather than an open [public] meeting), I would have remained quiet and simply passed out copies of my memos and emails to the First Chief and the rest of the Tribal Council showing that the First Chief's charge wasn't true. A glance at the first sentence or two would confirm to each person what I had already done and arranged on this matter (since they had already seen the original memo or email).

But this was a public meeting with tribal members who were not privy to my work and my memos to the Tribal Council.

So when the First Chief was finished with her tirade, I responded by saying that what she said wasn't true, that I had talked with these people, that they were willing to work with us, and that they had been prepared to meet with us at this very meeting.

*****

Several days later, in a discussion with another chief, he castigated me for responding to the First Chief's false statements. This chief was from both worlds (Native and White), and thereby knew both cultures. He said he knew that what I had done – "to speak truth to power", to confront false and misleading statements – was fine in my culture, but that it was considered "crossing swords" in their culture.

Such was not to be done here.

What was right did not matter.

The truth did not matter here.

Drunken Indian

(A Walk Down Along the Yukon)

"Drunken Indian", while possibly a true description of a particular person, is simply a term I don't like.

One day I was walking down along the Yukon River. Up ahead was a parked pickup, with two Indians inside it.

I'm short. I'm small. I have learned to avert, or defuse, dangerous situations.

As I was approaching the pickup, walking on the opposite side of the road, the drunken Indian in the driver's seat yelled out "Fighting Words", legalese for something provocative, something meant to inflame, to incite a fight.

Well, I wasn't provoked. I wasn't inflamed. In the flood of calculations the brain makes while quickly processing the "Flight or Fight" response[9] (whether it is with respect to a grizzly bear [as in "Silvertip Grizzly with Spirit Dog"] or with respect to a person as here), I decided [*in this instance*] to approach the driver's window.

The passenger in the pickup saw me, recognized me, and slapped the arm of the driver: ~ Hey! – What's wrong with you? – He's our boss! [I was the Executive Director of their Tribe (see "Chief No Feathers & His Loyal Scout Muddy Paws").]

The Drunken Indian turned on a dime: "Beautiful day", he said: "How are you doing?"

"Fine", I said as I looked in at the two Indians. "Yes, you're right, it is beautiful", and I nodded hello to both of them.

---

[9] You know the theory: you have milliseconds to determine how you are going to respond to a situation that will most likely end your life in the next few seconds [*if not sooner*]. Also see, e.g., "Silvertip Grizzly With Spirit Dog".

Yukon River Boat Races

Yukon River racing boats

Getting Ready

One boat is off & running while the crew for another boat gets prepared.

The "Rooster Tail" on the racing boat is starting to grow.

Yukon River racing boats seemed to be home-made affairs.

Perhaps they had to be, given the economics of the region and the terrain [the water – *The Yukon*] they had to contend with. They were certainly not factory manufactured.

Most were essentially 2 pieces of plywood attached end-to-end. The sidewalls were about 4" – 6" high. At the back end was attached an outboard motor [that did come from some factory "Outside"].

At the front end, in part to counterbalance the weight of the motor, and in part for safety, sat a "lookout" who scoured the river for dead-heads [dead trees, stumps and logs racing thousands of miles from deep inside Canada [starting somewhere up in the Klondike gold fields], down past The Fort, till the Yukon dumped its load into the Pacific] and for the constantly changing sand and gravel bars. Navigation on the Yukon in one summer therefore is different from navigation on the same stretch of water the next summer (or simply later in the summer). [Winter navigation, on snowmobile on the ice[10], is generally the same from year-to-year – just different risks.]

---

[10] See "Navigable Waters".

In the back sat the driver who steered the affair with either a wheel or holding on to the throttle handle on the outboard motor.

*****

It didn't look particularly safe to me.

*****

It isn't.

*****

But people on the Yukon look out for one another. That is the difference – the difference which changes a dangerous situation into a survivable one. Most people make it back alive.[11]

*****

Snowmobiles are meant to race, as the name implies, on snow. Or ice.

It has treads which go round on a belt very fast, allowing the snowmobile to travel very fast.

When it comes to water, most people wait for the water to freeze before taking a snowmobile out on to it.

But this is The Fort.

People do things differently out here.

*****

Yukon River boat races are timed events – that is, each boat leaves at different times, . . . whenever the crew wants to. The "winner" is the one who completes the course [down river, up river, and back] in the least amount of time. Most can do the course in a [summertime] "Arctic day". (If help needs to be sent out, it could take several days.)

*****

During an interval between race starts, I heard the distinct sound of a . . . snowmobile – how odd, particularly in the middle of July. I looked over and saw it on the bank of the Yukon, about a quarter mile upriver.

Then with a huge gulp of gas, a cloud of sand was launched behind it, and the snowmobile took off and leapt over the embankment and onto the river. The driver kept the snowmobile at full throttle. With the treads on the snowmobile belt whipping around incredibly fast, several hundred pounds of metal and a driver having some insane sense of fun raced out and about on top of the Yukon out in front of all of us, sending up a huge spray of water behind him.

---

[11] The motor on one of the racing boats broke down up river with one of the Tribal Council members I worked with on it. It took two days for him and his crew to get back to the Fort.

He did a couple of wide turns, and then decided to head in where sand had been brought in so the kids could wade out into the river without their feet slipping and getting ripped up by the rocks. When the mothers on the shore realized the snowmobiler was headed in straight for their children, they screamed, ran out and caught their child, and then ran back to the shore with their kid under their arms or clutched in their hands.

A glimpse of sanity broke through to the snowmobiler who saw all the mothers scrambling to get their kids away from his intended landing zone. He started to do "figure S's" to slow down his approach.

He succeeded.

About 50 feet offshore, where the depth of the Yukon was perhaps 10 feet, without sufficient speed to stay aloft, the snowmobile and its driver sank into the river. Both went out of sight.

While we stood on shore a bit aghast at what had just happened, trying to recover from one danger, and now trying to determine how to respond to the next one, the driver came flying up out of the water!

He had apparently touched bottom, and with an intense effort, used both legs to launch himself upwards.

Bursting out of the water, he slapped it and laughed his head off.[12]

$$*****$$

---

[12] As I've said elsewhere, people look at things differently than me [see, for example, "Crossing Swords"]. For me, he had just ruined a $10,000 snowmobile – but for him, it was just another great day on the Yukon!

One of the ladies turned from the river and, holding her i-phone above her head, told the crowd further up on the shore: ~ It's all [over the world] on You Tube now!

Tundra Drums

When I was planning to leave the Fort, at first only a few people [the Tribal Council and me] knew about it.

> *[N: there are no newspapers at the Fort, so news gets around by the modern equivalent of the "Tundra Drums" – via Public Radio up and down the Yukon.]*

So that is how Tribal Members who were then out at their family fish camps on the Yukon River (catching, smoking and drying Yukon River Salmon to keep them and their families alive and nourished for the long, dark, coming winter) first heard the news.

Some Tribal Members when they came back to the Fort (or never left it) would see me walking through town. They would cross the street, some to give me a hug, to say how thankful they were that I had come to the Fort.

They all knew (or could easily find out) where I lived, so some evenings when I came home from work I would find that they had left some Native foods [usually smoked and dried Yukon River Salmon] on my steps.

> A gift of "Thank you!"

About the Author (Chief No Feathers)

Chief No Feathers & His Loyal Scout Muddy Paws

At the end of the Indian Wars out West, photographers from the East went out to photograph a disappearing way of life, if not quite a disappearing people.

[I have always known this photograph existed –

I had just never seen it before now.]

Sioux encampment on the Great Plains of the American Midwest[13]

---

[13] Can you tell which way the prevailing wind is blowing?

I saw this with seagulls in a parking lot in Delaware over a century later (except the seagulls were facing *into* the wind).

The Sioux have their smoke flaps set so that the smoke from the fires within their tipis (to keep them warm and to cook their food), [and so that the drafts for those fires are better and stronger] . . . blows away from their camp.

The "savages" at least knew what they were doing.

Some of the photographers concentrated on the people, their tipis and their camps, while others concentrated on taking portraits of their chiefs.

One of these portraits was of Chief Two Feathers.

I have no idea who Chief Two Feathers was, what his claim to fame might have been, or how he might have earned the two feathers. All I know is that there is a photograph of him.

*****

While working for the Tribe at the Fort, I was severely injured, with the injury requiring major surgery. When I went back about a week later to have the stitches removed from the various incisions, I was talking to the assistant surgeon. He asked what I did. I said I was the Executive Director of a tribe, but I didn't know if I was the Chief non-chief, or a non-chief Chief.

The surgeon, earlier in his career, like many doctors in Alaska, had worked out in the Bush in various villages, and knew of the tenuous and fluctuating reality of tribal power. I told him that while the staff and tribal members preferred to call me "Boss" (their term – not a term of my choosing), that there were real, but unspoken, limits to my authority.

~ Oh, said the surgeon, so you're like a chief with no feathers.

— Exactly – Chief No Feathers!

Little Miss Bella has just put her right front paw on Captain Sparky's back,
so he is about to react. (Blue huckleberries can be seen growing behind Sparky's tail.)

Golden colored fish can be seen in the pond behind the puppies.
(They were all subsequently wiped out by being eaten by Snapping Turtles
[see "The Prehistoric Creature With The Dinosaur Tail"].)

I had several projects going on at the Lower Pond, including building a dam to raise the water level of the pond, and a deck (see above) so we could go out over the pond and look down at the fish swimming by below. Captain Sparky and Little Miss Bella would be out there with me while I worked and they played. Shih Tzu's are not water dogs like Spaniels, so do not go out to swim. But they do recognize water for the purposes of drinking, and freely did so. While Little Miss Bella could do so without getting all messy, Sparky had a way of always finding the mud – hence his well-earned nickname: "Muddy Paws".

So when it was time for a break, and we'd go out to explore the forest, it was Chief No Feathers and his loyal scout Muddy Paws who went out with Little Miss Bella to see what the forest had in store for us that day.

Made in the USA
Monee, IL
07 July 2026

56552462R00024